T0201690

CLAWS

THIS EDITION
Editorial Management by Oriel Square
Produced for DK by WonderLab Group LLC
Jennifer Emmett, Erica Green, Kate Hale, *Founders*

Editors Grace Hill Smith, Libby Romero, Michaela Weglinski;
Photography Editors Kelley Miller, Annette Kiesow, Nicole di Mella; **Managing Editor** Rachel Houghton;
Designers Project Design Company; **Researcher** Michelle Harris; **Copy Editor** Lori Merritt;
Indexer Connie Binder; **Proofreader** Larry Shea; **Reading Specialist** Dr. Jennifer Albro;
Curriculum Specialist Elaine Larson

Published in the United States by DK Publishing
1745 Broadway, 20th Floor, New York, NY 10019
Copyright © 2023 Dorling Kindersley Limited
DK, a Division of Penguin Random House LLC
23 24 25 26 10 9 8 7 6 5 4 3 2 1
001-333981-June/2023

A catalog record for this book
is available from the Library of Congress.
HC ISBN: 978-0-7440-7302-7
PB ISBN: 978-0-7440-7303-4

DK books are available at special discounts when purchased in bulk for sales promotions, premiums,
fundraising, or educational use. For details, contact: DK Publishing Special Markets,
1745 Broadway, 20th Floor, New York, NY 10019
SpecialSales@dk.com

Printed and bound in China

The publisher would like to thank the following for their kind permission to reproduce their images:
a=above; c=center; b=below; l=left; r=right; t=top; b/g=background

Alamy Stock Photo: A & J Visage 12cr, Avalon.red / Photoshot 11t, blickwinkel / Hummel 22br, Holger Ehlers 9t, imageBROKER /
Thorsten Negro 12t, Images of Africa Photobank / David Keith Jones 8br; **Dorling Kindersley:** Lynette Schimming 19tl;
Dreamstime.com: Rinus Baak 26bl, Mikhail Blajenov / Starper 19tr, Tony Bosse 24t, Liliya Butenko 28cl, Vladimir Cech 18b,
Dwiputra18 10b, Rudolf Ernst 13br, Gatito33 25cr, Eugen Haag 13tc, Isselee 3cb, Geoffrey Kuchera 7br, Holly Kuchera 4–5,
Pbardocz 13cl, Zuzana Randlova 14br, Seadam 1cb, Lisa F. Young 18cra, Rudmer Zwerver 24br; **Getty Images:** The Image Bank /
Kevin Schafer 28br, 29t, The Image Bank / Martin Harvey 20c; **Getty Images / iStock:** DC_Colombia 22tl, dstephens 21cr,
Otografias 6t, sdominick 30bc, Stefonlinton 21tl; **naturepl.com:** Flip de Nooyer 26tr, 27t; **Shutterstock.com:** Charlotte Heijmans 23,
Penty Photography 17cra, phugunfire 15, Milan Zygmunt 16–17t

Cover images: *Front:* **Dreamstime.com:** Cat Vec ca/ (x3), Seadam; *Back:* **Dreamstime.com:** Pavel Naumov clb;
Spine: **Dreamstime.com:** Seadam

All other images © Dorling Kindersley
For more information see: www.dkimages.com

For the curious
www.dk.com

CLAWS

Ruth A. Musgrave

Contents

Claws

Meow! This kitty's got claws. Many animals have claws.

Claws help animals run, climb, and dig. Claws help animals find food and protect themselves. Claws are handy survival tools.

What is a claw? Look at this kitten's claws. Now look at your nails. Do you see the difference? Nails are usually flat and short. Claws are curved and long. They are also strong and often sharp.

Whether an animal has claws or nails depends on many things, like where it lives, what it eats, and what it needs to survive. People do not need claws. You might like to climb trees, but your survival probably doesn't depend on it. Animals like black bears need claws. Claws help bears rip into rotten logs to find food or scamper up a tree to escape danger.

Ready to claw your way through this book to discover animals with the coolest claws?

Black Bear
A black bear's claws can be as long as your second toe. The whole toe, not just the nail on your toe!

Lion

Moving almost silently on its big padded paws, the lion creeps forward. It keeps its eyes on the prize, a zebra that has wandered from its herd.

In a burst of speed, the lion races through the tall grass, catching the zebra. The big cat sinks its sharp claws into the prey.

A lion's claws work like a secret weapon. Some animals' claws stick out all the time, like a bear's or your dog's. But cats can pull in their claws. This ability allows the cats to walk quietly and keeps their claws from wearing down. The claws instantly pop out when needed.

Extra Claw

Lions have a dew claw on each of their front paws that sits higher on their legs. The dew claw works like a sharp thumb, helping cats grab and hold onto their prey.

dew claw

Lions scratch trees to keep their claws sharp.

A lion's claws may not be the longest in the world, but they are attached to the powerful paws and legs of a strong cat. They all work together to quickly take down prey.

Flying Squirrel

A squirrel looks for food in a tree. **Yikes!** It spots a predator instead and races up a branch. What should it do? If it's a flying squirrel, it can fly away.

A flying squirrel has a flap of skin between its front and back legs. The squirrel leaps from the tree. It holds out its legs. The flaps catch air, like a parachute. The squirrel glides away. It aims for the side of a tree. The squirrel's claws latch onto the bark and dig in.

These claws might not look as powerful as a lion's or bear's claws, but could you cling to the side of the tree with just your nails? Probably not for long. This squirrel's claws sound pretty powerful now, don't they?

Watch out! Owl at two o'clock! Flying squirrels can make sharp turns to avoid flying predators.

Aye-aye

Tap, tap. Tap, tap.
Listen. The aye-aye drums
the log with its long, skinny, clawed finger.

Its big ears listen for tiny tunnels made by insects. When it hears a hollow sound, it chews into the wood. Then, the aye-aye digs its long finger deep inside the skinny tunnel. The curved claw hooks and pulls out an insect. Dinner is served!

Africa

Aye-ayes only live
in Madagascar, an
island country off
the southeastern
coast of Africa.

Madagascar

Grooming Claw
Meet a cleaning, climbing
machine. Some primates
have special claws to clean
their fur. It is called a
grooming claw or a toilet claw.

Southern Cassowary

The bright colors on a cassowary's face and neck will make you smile. But don't laugh. This serious bird is seriously dangerous.

A cassowary has three razor-sharp claws on each foot. One of the claws is four inches (10 cm) long! A powerful strike with its claws can slice an animal open. The cassowary's claws make it one of the most dangerous animals in the world.

This tall bird is not a predator, though. It eats fruit. A cassowary would rather disappear into the rainforest than fight. But it will charge and kick when threatened.

Headgear
Scientists think the cassowary's cool headgear might help the bird lose heat when it gets too hot.

Males are about as tall or taller than most human adults.

Sloth

Hanging right side up or upside down from a branch is just another day in the rainforest for a sloth. These animals eat, sleep, and even have babies while hanging by all four feet.

Harpy eagles (see page 22) hunt sloths. Sloths lash out with their claws to protect themselves.

Bone and Keratin

A sloth's claws are made of bone that is covered with keratin. The claws will regrow if they break. A sloth's claws can be four inches (10 cm) long. If your nails were as long as a sloth's, you could stand and scratch your knees without bending over!

When you hang onto a branch, your hands quickly become tired. That's because you use muscles to hold on. But a sloth's claws are relaxed when it hangs. That means the sloth doesn't use any energy to grip a branch.

Sloth Bear

Sniff. Snort. Snuffle. Grunt. Slurp. These are the sounds of a sloth bear searching for food. It eats termites, ants, and bees. This animal's wonderful sense of smell helps it find insects wherever they hide.

The claws don't stop the sloth bear from running fast. It can run faster than you.

termite mound

Nose Closed
A sloth bear closes its nostrils when it eats to stop bees or termites from climbing into its nose.

Look at its claws! They are perfect for digging, climbing, ripping apart wood, and breaking into termite mounds. A termite mound isn't just a pile of dirt. It's a tiny mountain built with mud, spit, and sometimes poop. Millions of termites can live inside this sturdy mound.

A sloth bear's long, strong claws crack into the mound. Imagine ripping into a giant, hard box with your bare hands to get your lunch!

Once the mound is open, the bear puckers its lips and sucks in the bugs. Yum!

Cat Claw Comparison

Many kinds of wild cats live around the world in deserts, mountains, and forests. Cats use their claws to hunt and survive. But not all cats use their claws in the same way. Meet three awesome cats that each use their claws in different ways.

Serval
Fishhooks for claws? A serval's curved claws hook fish and frogs. They also snag rats hiding inside burrows.

Cheetah

Speed and agility are everything to a cheetah. Its claws work like the spikes on the bottom of soccer shoes, gripping the ground as the cat runs fast. They help the cat make sharp turns as it chases prey.

Margay

A climbing cat isn't so unusual. But this cat is the tree-climbing champion. A margay spends most of its time in trees. It can hang by just one of its clawed paws. Most cats that climb a tree either jump down or shimmy down tail first. Margays can turn their ankles around and use their claws to walk down headfirst.

Harpy Eagle

Few animals can escape the bone-crushing power of a harpy eagle's claws and feet. A harpy eagle is one of the largest and most powerful eagles in the world.

It is as tall as a five-year-old child. Its legs are as thick as your wrist. Its claws are as long as a grizzly bear's claws.

The eagle perches in rainforest trees. It watches and waits for prey. Then, it quickly and silently swoops through the branches. It grabs prey with its powerful clawed feet, and then carries it into a tree to eat. Monkeys and sloths are a big part of the eagle's diet. These eagles also eat opossums, iguanas, and snakes.

Its wingspan can be more than six feet (1.8 m) wide.

Harpy Helmet

Harpy eagles don't hunt or attack people. That is, unless people climb trees to film the bird's babies. Scientists had to wear motorcycle helmets to stay safe while filming in the trees.

Badger

Badgers don't run like cheetahs. They can't snatch animals from trees like harpy eagles, but they sure can dig.

Badgers are one of the fastest-digging mammals in the world. Long claws and powerful arms help a badger dig faster than a person using a shovel.

Badgers eat prairie dogs, squirrels, gophers, mice, and other animals.

A badger uses its digging skills to hunt. It searches for animals hiding in their underground homes. It blocks the entrance with dirt. Then, it quickly digs a new entrance to catch the trapped prey inside.

Badgers also use their claws to bury food to eat later. They scrape loose dirt on top so other animals cannot find the leftovers.

Snack for Later
Webcam video caught a badger taking five days to bury a cow carcass. The badger buried the dead animal so well that it left no evidence behind. Scientists didn't know anything had been buried until they watched the video.

Hoatzin

Belly flop!
These baby hoatzins (HWAT-seens) drop from a tree into the water when a snake gets too close. Their parents build the nests above water. That way, the birds can save themselves by diving into the water.

These baby birds have claws on their feet, like other birds. But unlike most other birds, they also have claws sticking out of their wings.

Stinkbirds
Hoatzins are stinky birds that burp a lot. Some people call them stinkbirds.

wing claw

The chick waits until it is safe to move. Then, it uses its wings to swim to shore. This is where its unique wing claws come into play. The chick climbs up the tree using both its wing claws and the claws on its feet, just like a four-legged animal would. Chicks lose their wing claws when they grow up.

Giant Armadillo

The giant armadillo wins the coolest claw contest. It has the longest claws in the world. A three-foot (0.9-m)-long giant armadillo's claws are nearly eight inches (20 cm) long.

Giant armadillos walk on the tips of their giant claws. They use them to crack open termite mounds and to dig for ants.

The winner of the longest claws of all time belonged to the plant-eating *Therizinosaurus*. Its claws were about three feet (1 m) long. That's as long as a three-year-old child is tall. This dino used its supersize claws to slash predators.

Bony Plates

Armadillos are mammals with a "shell." The shell is made of bony plates covered with thick skin. Scales cover an armadillo's head, legs, and tail.

Giant armadillos' camouflage keeps them hidden from predators—and scientists. These secretive animals are rarely seen.

. . . .

Whether they rip, tear, climb, dig, dash, or slash, claws help animals survive. Now that you've clawed your way through this book, which animal would you want to be?

Glossary

Aye-aye
A small primate related to monkeys and apes

Burrow
A tunnel that animals dig to live in

Keratin
[care-ah-tin]
The material that makes up an animal's hair and nails

Prehistoric
A long time ago before humans had written records

Prey
An animal hunted by other animals

Predator
An animal that hunts other animals

Rainforest
A kind of forest filled with trees that gets a lot of rain

Termites
Small insects that live in large groups inside mounds or underground

Therizinosaurus
A dinosaur that lived about 80 million years ago

Index

Quiz

Answer the questions to see what you have learned. Check your answers in the key below.

1. How does a flying squirrel use its claws?

2. Which animal taps to find its food?

3. True or False: A cassowary uses its claws to catch its food.

4. Name two animals that use their claws to hang in trees.

5. What does a sloth bear eat?

6. What big clawed animal hunts prairie dogs?

7. What baby bird has claws on its wings?

8. What living animal has the longest claws?

1. To cling to trees 2. Aye-aye 3. False 4. Sloths and margays
5. Termites, ants, and bees 6. Badger 7. Hoatzin 8. Giant armadillo